MAKE YOUR OWN APPLICATION

Cats, Kids, and Christ

Michael Newnham

Reader Hill
Yucaipa, California

MAKE YOUR OWN APPLICATION: CATS, KIDS, AND CHRIST
Copyright © 2012, 2015 by Michael Newnham
www.michaelnewnham.com

ALL RIGHTS RESERVED. No part of this text may be reproduced, stored in a retrieval system, scanned, or transmitted, in any form or by any means, electronic, mechanical, photocopying, recording, or otherwise without prior written permission of the publisher. The only exception is the reproduction of brief quotations as part of a review of this work.

Much of the material in this book was originally published in 2012 as
MAKE YOUR OWN APPLICATION
Copyright © 2012 by Michael Newnham

Cover design and interior formatting by Public Author
Front cover photo copyright © Alexander Kharchenko | Dreamstime.com
Interior and back cover photos copyright © Michael Newnham

Scripture quotations marked (ESV) are from the ESV® Bible (The Holy Bible, English Standard Version®), copyright © 2001 by Crossway, a publishing ministry of Good News Publishers. Used by permission. All rights reserved.

Scripture quotations marked (THE MESSAGE) are from THE MESSAGE. Copyright © by Eugene H. Peterson 1993, 1994, 1995, 1996, 2000, 2001, 2002. Used by permission of NavPress. All rights reserved. Represented by Tyndale House Publishers, Inc.

Published by
Reader Hill
PO Box 490
Yucaipa, CA 92399-0490
www.readerhill.com

Reader Hill logo and colophon are trademarks of Reader Hill.

Dedication

This book is dedicated to Brian Daugherty, Noelle Pellett Nazami, Dusty Morgan, and Sarah Mossman Wolfe, without whom there would be no Phoenix Preacher. Their friendship, support, and prayers have served me and our online community in ways most will not know until we get home.

Make Your Own Application- Book 1

Introduction to the Series

Welcome to the **Make Your Own Application** series of devotionals by Michael Newnham. Michael is a dad, pastor, blogger, and author who takes a unique approach to learning from God. He looks for God's lessons in those every-day, ordinary, sometimes-surprising, sometimes-frustrating, normal things that make up our daily lives. He finds the wonder and he shares it with us.

Be forewarned, there are some things that you will **not** find in this devotional. There are no daily prayers to recite, no checklists of things to do to improve your holiness, and there certainly aren't any fill-in-the-blank sections demanding your pat answers. This isn't that kind of study. You won't even find any mandatory scripture verses to memorize. No, **Make Your Own Application** is a devotional that's something entirely different. It is meant to be an open discovery of God's truths for life.

You will, however, find one requirement when reading this book. You will be encouraged after each reading to "make your own application." Please do so.

This book is divided into Days, but that is merely for your convenience. Read this book as quickly or as slowly as you wish. We just hope that you will find it spiritually challenging, as well as encouraging in your Christian walk.

In Book 1 of this series- CATS, KIDS, and CHRIST- you will discover the spiritual lessons to be found in the most ordinary events in life, from parenting to caring for a sick cat, from sharing your faith to facing the loss of a job.

* * *

Some may wonder the history behind the writing of the **Make Your Application** study series. Well, here's Michael to tell you how these devotionals came into existence:

> About six years ago, I started writing a weekly column on Fridays I cleverly called "TGIF". What actually happened was that I woke up one Friday morning and had no idea what to write. Suddenly, something fell out of my head and onto the keyboard. It had to have a title… and it was Friday, after all.
>
> After some hits and misses, I found my voice writing about what was going on in my daily life and drawing scriptural applications from the same. I wrote about my son and the skateboard park, I wrote about my doubts, I wrote about my faith… and I wrote about my cats. Miss Kitty and Squeak became regular guests of my readers, as I chronicled how God speaks through critters. This book is a collection of those writings.
>
> My prayer is that they will bless you and cause you to think… and make your own applications.
>
> - Michael Newnham

Make Your Own Application- Book 1

Kids

From the mouth of babes...

The other day, my son Trey said, "Sometimes I think I believe in God just so I won't go to hell."

I've failed to give him as many reasons to live for Christ as to die in Him. That... is grave error.

Michael Newnham

Come and Drink

DAY 1

Every day for the last two summers, Trey and I have loaded up an ice chest full of water and pop and headed to a local skate park. The refreshments are available for anyone, the only requirement being that you are thirsty.

You don't have to ask for permission and you don't have to say thank you…you just come and drink.

The back of my truck stays open and people are free to come and get what they need…and they have come in large numbers.

The young ones,

The older ones,

The skaters,

The scooters,

The bikers,

The clean ones,

The dirty ones,

The straight ones and the stoners.

The only ones who won't come are the ones who don't like

my son or me. They will refuse to come no matter how hot, dry, and parched they are…they will sit on the concrete flushed with heat and suffer before they will walk to the truck for relief.

Sometimes, when I see this, I'll walk over and silently offer a bottle of ice water plucked from the chest…and it's usually refused with a glare. They will try to find someone else's water to drink and failing that will trudge off to find something to relieve them somewhere.

It's hard to watch and hard to understand…we would freely give them what they need, if they would just come and receive it. I keep thinking that if they knew how much we cared, they would be able to care back and enjoy their time that much more. That's a lot to ask for some people…to believe that someone cares and will freely give them what they need.

Sometimes, it's too much to ask.

Make your own application…

The Missing Part

DAY 2

The back of my SUV is a rolling skateboard shop on wheels.

We have the ice chest full of ice, water, and soda.

We have the big first aid kit with ice packs, bandages, Neosporin, gauze, and tape.

We have spares…spare helmets, spare pads, spare nuts, spare bolts, spare wheels, and spare tools to put all the spare parts on the boards as need be.

We have almost everything all the kids need to enjoy a hot summer day at the skate park without incident…with spares to boot.

Almost everything.

We are consistently missing the most vital thing the kids need to fully enjoy the experience.

I've looked at all the parks and can't find any.
I've gone to the skate shops and can't find any.

I can't order any, I can't buy any, I just can't find any... though I have proof they exist.

We are desperately short of fathers.

I don't think the kids misplaced them or lost them intentionally, but the fact is that many of them usually can't find theirs.

Some of them have given up looking for them.

We have some moms that are bravely trying to replace them, but it's not the same and they are showing signs of pressure cracks.

I can replace the nuts and bolts and bearings and wheels so that equipment works...I can put Band-Aids on wounds and ice packs on sprains...but I can't replace that one missing part.

I can fix the board, but the rider stays broken.

I don't have any spare dads.

If you find one, please send him down to the skate park...or the school...or maybe even home.

There are some broken things only he can fix.

Make your own application...

Social Media?

DAY 3

I'm now well into my second year of daily forced attendance at our local skateboarding parks and I have made some observations that I should probably keep to myself, but as usual, I won't. I will grant at the outset that my observations are taken from a limited demographic economically and socially, if that disclaimer makes you feel better.

My **first observation** is that our youth are self-medicating at about the same rate the rest of the population is.

We had to leave parks twice in the last week because of eleven and twelve year olds choking me out with marijuana smoke. This displeased me greatly because I do not self-medicate with marijuana, I use traditional non-prescription methods, which I believe are morally superior to weed. Some of the youth use my methods as well, as we found out when one of them got drunk and drowned in the creek last month.

Self-medication is a reaction to those (usually undefined) cultural and societal pains and stresses that cause us great discomfort and anxiety… and our kids have been swept up in the plague.

The **second observation** I would make is that kids are sexually active and emotionally hardened to the implications of that at an age when I was still learning to spell the word "sexually" and had only a rudimentary knowledge of what the word meant.

The **third observation** I would like to share this morning is that if Jesus comes back, he will need business cards after the pyrotechnics because most of the kids I have met have no real idea who He is.

Satan, however, has a better advance team and is well known and appreciated by many.

It seems that while we have been busy tweeting and blogging and Facebooking to make ourselves known to each other, we have neglected to display Jesus to the unbelieving market with the same fervor.

Perhaps the Lord should buy a Mac and learn to tweet.
I heard He has a book out.

Make your own application…

Give a Little

Day 4

It's been hot… so I'm used to hearing the back door of my truck open and close repeatedly. I heard it close again and knew it was probably time to get up and put some more water bottles in the ice chest. What I saw instead of a thirsty skater was an elderly woman holding a bottle of our water on the back of her neck.

She looked afraid… and ready to pass out.

"They said it was free…"

"It is."

Seems she had walked to the store and had underestimated both the distance and the temperature… and asked the kids where they got their water when she was shuffling by.

I gave her my chair and she revived enough to finish her little journey… thankful to God for giving her some unexpected refreshment.

* * *

When I got home Miss Kitty was waiting… for dinner.

I fed her and sat down at the computer and the cat jumped into my lap.

A different cat.

A cat I had never seen before.

Ever.

She was a very thin cat with a squeak where a meow should be and I understand cat and squeak well enough to know she was hungry.

I fed her… then she hopped on my bed, took a bath, and then went back to wherever she came from in the first place.

An hour later two other cats were sitting outside my door… and the squeaky lap cat strolled past them into her new home that I didn't know I had invited her to live in.

I fed all three… and pondered how cats network.

My conclusion from these events is this…if one will open their hearts to meet a need, no matter how small or insignificant it may seem… God will use that opening to bless far more people (or cats or dogs or badgers) than you expected, far more than you expected them to be blessed.

If you don't, they won't.

As always, you can make your own application.

Learn to Fly

Day 5

"Your kid is amazing…he can really fly."

I acknowledged his compliment whilst hoping he would move on after his kind words.

"My kid can't get the hang of this, I don't know what his problem is."

Now I knew he wasn't going anywhere soon.

"Do you have any advice? … He's the same age as your son and wants to do what he does."

I set down my iPad and watched his boy for a minute and the problem was obvious. "Buy him some pads."

"Why? He's never hurt himself."

"The proper equipment will give him the confidence to risk falling down… because he will know that he'll be able to get back up and try again."

I then added, "He's afraid to fall… and he will never fly until he's not afraid to fall… and that's the Gospel truth".

* * *

I'm so dense it took me ten minutes to understand that what I said really is the Gospel truth… and that the blood of Christ has provided us with a full set of pads and a custom helmet.

Falling is in our nature, flying is our inheritance, and fear will always keep you grounded.

Make your own application… You're safe.

Killing Snakes

Day 6

Tough day at the skate park yesterday. First, I look up from my book and my kid is lying crumpled on the concrete. It wasn't serious, "just" a badly mangled elbow and he declined my medical ministrations and chose to keep skating. About fifteen minutes later he is yelling at the top of his lungs for me to come help someone else.

This was serious…

I'll spare you the graphic description, but one of the kids hurt his leg badly and was taken away in an ambulance. When the boy was gone and the crisis over… the skating commenced again.
Welcome to Life 101.

Trey is usually a mass of bruises in different stages of healing and various shades of purple. Despite this, he finds joy in his daily journey to ride a plank of wood on wheels.
One day I fear he will hurt himself badly… he accepts that risk as being part of experiencing the joy.

* * *

We've met some great people while skating… and we've met some real scoundrels.

We've met people who helped us learn and grow and we've met people who would injure you on purpose… both on the same day. The big guys will run you over on purpose sometimes… it's called getting "snaked".

That's a very appropriate term.

* * *

At the end of the day… it's about the **joy.**

Some of us in the church are bruised… some of us got hurt badly and decided that joy wasn't worth the risk. Some of us still go to the park and do a running commentary on how dangerous it is and how bad the people were who hurt us and there are snakes, snakes, everywhere.

We got snaked… and we want to tell all the people pursuing joy that they will get snaked too… because we've lost our joy and seeing joy when you don't have it is like getting snaked over and over again.

Joy is a choice… a choice to pursue that which brings joy despite living in a snake pit.

The other alternative is to lead a joyless life and spend it trying to convince others to be joyless too.

I'm going to follow my nine-year-old's example… and seek joy despite the pain that is both familiar and inevitable.

Joy is worth it.

Make your own application.

Christian Community

If you saw a person walking through a store punching himself , kicking himself, and spitting on himself, you would think him either sick or insane... yet that's what we are doing when we hate another part of the Body of Christ.

* * *

When the church emulates the world it contributes to the decline of both.

* * *

The one who picks up the cross to follow Jesus will be crushed beneath it if they are not in a community that bears each other's burdens...

The Presence of the Father

Day 7

Trey was laid out on the concrete in obvious pain. I looked up, assessed the damage, and went back to reading my book.

The mother of another child rushed out to tend to him… I observed her and went back to reading my book.

He started to get up… and she rushed over to me to loudly rebuke my parenting skills and judge my heart as a father. I let her vent… and calmly informed her that I'm always here and I always know how bad he's hurt and when I need to intervene.

She wasn't satisfied… but Trey is not her child.

We decided a couple of years ago to let him get involved in an activity where he is guaranteed to get hurt every day. And he does. We provide as much protection as we can for his body and we are always present in case we're needed.

He is free to make decisions about the tricks he attempts to do and how fast or recklessly, or wisely, he wants to ride.

I provide him with as much guidance and counsel as I am able... and he is free to listen and apply it or ignore it.

When he really needs help he calls me, and if he doesn't call me I just observe in silence. There are times when he should call on me, but he doesn't...

He skates in community and in that community are some who will help him grow, some who will hurt him on purpose, and the majority who don't bother doing either.

He is bruised and scraped from head to toe and always will be as long as he chooses to skate. He is also full of joy and excitement at the beginning of each day's skating and throughout the day the payoff is greater than the pain. At the end of each day, he's learned something new and enjoyed the process of learning it, even though there were some crashes and falls on the way.

His father is always present, always concerned, always ready to help, and usually quiet.

Always present.

Always.

Make your own application...

Christian Witness

Nothing will cripple your witness faster than having to be "right". Learned that from a *friend*, I lied out loud...

* * *

You can assess how much you believe in the grace of God by determining how much you want the person you despise the most to receive it.

Therapy

Day 8

Every year we get together with Trey's teachers to determine what programs he will be in and what special help he will need to succeed in school. We did this last week and we were discussing the new therapy we have him in called "neuro feedback."

They hook him up with electrodes and have him hold a teddy bear that monitors his vital signs while he looks at a video game monitor. The game is controlled completely by the mind…and teaches him how to control his thoughts and reactions. It's very high tech and very expensive, but very effective. There is only one other aspect to the therapy and we enlisted his teachers to apply it as well.

Hugs.

Asperger's kids have a hard time feeling "connected" to their bodies, so they need firm hugs frequently.

The teacher's reactions were telling… they lit up… and a formal hearing became something very different when permission to hug was asked for and granted.

Evidently, others need this therapy as well.

You may need this therapy.

The need for hugs may well have reached epidemic proportions and I suspect we're sicker than we know.

Reach for the cure… and make your own application.

Cats

Dangling String

I was amazed at how smart my cat was, until I realized that she will play endlessly with a piece of string that's obviously dangling from my hand. Then I went and watched my Twitter feed and realized I'm not so bright myself...

Michael Newnham

Unconditional Love

Day 9

The cat was basically long hair and bones, a living transport vehicle for fleas and yard debris. It was bold enough to stick its head in the door and ask for food, so I fed it while it unloaded some of its passengers.

It was the Christian thing to do.

It came back and Trey grew fond of it because it tolerated Trey and most cats don't.

The cat decided that between 2:00 AM and 3:AM was the appropriate time on her schedule for us to have a snack and bond… and I dutifully did so for two nights.

On the third night, the cat jumped on the bed and began to nuzzle and weave and I decided that I only wanted to be nuzzled and wove by something with less hair and fewer insects… especially at 2:30 AM.

Did I mention I'm allergic to both cats and fleas?

The beast took this temporal rejection personally and stuck claws into each side of my head while sinking fangs right into the middle of my scalp.

Thus, Miss Kitty became the first cat in space.

The next day I told Trey that the beast had not only disturbed the felicity of my slumber, but had injured me and I damned the cat to feline perdition.

His response… "That cat is very important to me. I love that cat and no matter what it does, I will still love it."

Out of the mouths of babes… make your own application… I have to feed the cat.

Know Thyself

Day 10

Miss Kitty has an identity crisis. I came to this conclusion after picking out foxtails and burrs from her coat for an hour, then brushing out a thick coating of dirt and some sort of oil that was enabling said dirt to stick... to everything. She insists on living in the weeds under a boat across the street, even though I have prepared a clean, comfortable place for her to dwell.

She's the bag lady of the feline neighborhood.

She eats nervously and quickly... always looking about to see if the cat that really owns the food is going to come and attack her for eating purloined Whiskas. A few quick bites and back out to the weeds, never understanding that the feast set before her was all hers to enjoy... never understanding that her new master will allow no one to injure her for doing so.

She craves affection, but can only enjoy it for a moment before memories of owners past overwhelm her and she either lashes out or runs or both. Back to the dirt, back to the foxtails, back to the pain.

She doesn't get it.

Her address has been transferred from the street to a home and every blessing a cat could want is hers to freely enjoy.

I chose her.

I adopted her.

I have made a place and provision for her. I'll never hurt her.

She's loved, but she doesn't get it.

It's hell not to know who you are.

Make your own application…

Heavenly Pets

Day 11

I knew it would happen if I kept writing cat vignettes. I knew that the animal lovers would think they had found a kindred spirit who was also a preacher and they would write in large numbers, asking for a satisfying answer to the question that has vexed them.

I do so love the word "vexed".

I digress.

What I feared has come upon me and the question of course, is "Will my pet go to heaven?"

Are you crazy? Of course they will. (Although, some of my correspondents need to know that I'm sure their *pets* will make it, but I'm not certain that the *person* will ever be there to know that…)

The theologians in the crowd just passed out or spit,

depending on whether they have cat food in their kitchens.

My cat (she's my cat now, not the cat) just walked in and called for attention. I removed some painful burrs from her coat and fed her. She walked by my chair on the way out, put her paws on my lap and bumped her head against mine, then left.

That was obviously her saying thank you… she did everything but leave a tip. I think she would have done that as well, but unemployment is high here and her coat has no pockets anyway.

She showed intelligence, affection, and gratitude.

Our pets often outdo their owners in what we consider "godly" attributes. Their loyalty, love, and gratitude often exceed that which we receive from our own species. Those are God given virtues, they are not natural. Do not tell me that animals have no soul… they do not have a human soul, but they indeed have a soul.

They were present in the first creation, they will be present in the new creation, and the Bible celebrates them in the Millennium.

Do not trouble me with arcane questions about sin and redemption… the Bible says that creation is groaning, awaiting its redemption, and it will be redeemed. How God does this is beyond my pay scale and beyond my caring.

God created men and animals to have a unique relationship and to have the ability to bond in love. Those relationships and that love come from a common fountain and it springs eternal.

I will end with a quote from a real theologian, the esteemed Dr. Martin Luther speaking to his dog…

"Be thou comforted, little dog," he once said. "Thou too in Resurrection shall have a little golden tail."

Amen.

Getting Older

By its very nature, wisdom takes time to accumulate. When a culture refuses to either employ or listen to its older citizens it will be the opposite of wise...

* * *

Nursing homes and funeral homes were created so we wouldn't have to deal with reality in our own homes.

You Want What?

Day 12

Miss Kitty is impudent. Because Trey is fond of her, I have elected to provide for her kitty needs. This, despite the fact that I am allergic to her, allergies made worse by the fact that she's shedding her fur at the expected rate of someone wearing a hair coat in summer.

There is Miss Kitty hair everywhere… my pristine editions of Calvin's Institutes look like they are growing Calvin's beard.

She carries these sharp sticker things in her fur from the fields and these sticker things end up stuck in my bed and stuck in me later in the most tender of places.

I provide for her kitty needs despite the fact that she eats multiple times a day with the final fresh snack expected at around 2 AM. I am expected to rise and serve this immediately after being awakened by yowling that would be more appropriate if she was being pitchforked by the cat devil.

Michael Newnham

I have dutifully fulfilled my obligations.

These things however, are not what confound me.

What confounds me is that, despite all that I have done for this beast, she wants more. In addition to being fed, watered, and sheltered and defleaed, she wants me to… like her.

She wants attention and affection and time… and seems discontent when her advances are spurned.

The nerve of cats these days.
After all I've done…

Make your own application…

Garbage

Day 13

Cats don't always clean their plates so I find myself with a lot of half eaten, leftover, cat food. This is deposited under the plum tree… because the blue jays love it. (Yes, I feed birds too.)

What the birds don't eat decomposes back to the earth and during that process is… yucky.

It is garbage… slimy, ant-infested garbage.

Which brings me to a very nice orange and white cat that I call "Owl" because he has a round face and I find calling animals by the name of another species faintly amusing.

Owl will not stop eating that garbage food, even though I offer him fresh Whiskas on a clean plate.

He won't get that close… even though I know the other cats have told him I'm harmless.

His bad experiences are far more real to him than any positive potential.

Nonetheless, every day I set out a saucer of clean food and water for him... and every day he sits under the plum tree and eats garbage.

He thinks the plum tree is safe and the garbage is filling...he thinks his needs are being met, though I know he is often sick. He is not safe... the raccoon would kill him for the garbage he eats... and the raccoon is always lurking.

I've thought about not throwing out that excess food, but Owl would just find garbage to eat elsewhere.

It is a sad thing to see a creature fill itself with garbage when unpolluted food is available... and an enemy is ever present. It is sadder to become so used to garbage that you think garbage is good... and prefer it to that which is pure.

In time, either the garbage or the enemy will take its toll... unless I can love this cat back home.

Make your own application... and take out the garbage.

Finishing Badly

Day 14

Plato is not finishing well. He is past the twenty year mark in age... and in human years that means... well, it means he should have been dead a few years ago.

Sometimes, he looks like that happened and someone forgot to inform him he was deceased. He is stiff from arthritis and moves with great difficulty. His thyroid is shot and we have to empty his bladder for him... unless of course he tries to squeeze through the door and it empties out on the carpet.

He lives off being hand fed a supplement because he no longer will eat regular cat food.

Unless... the food is for another cat.

If he comes across food for another cat in his gimpy travels about the property he will greedily consume it as if he were young, fit, and had not yet been neutered.

If another cat tries to dine with him, he will act as if he will fight them on the spot... even though he's not steady enough to stay in the same spot for long without falling down.

He's a bitter cat.

This troubles me because Plato has enjoyed a fine feline existence. He has never wanted for anything, he has been well fed and cared for, and has even enjoyed the regular consumption of treats. He has been greatly loved and enjoyed a position of respect in the household.

Today, he does little but watch for other cats who used to be his friends and spits at them when they approach. He resents the fact that we share our affection with others and he loathes the fact that newly adopted cats get treated as well as he does.

His health isn't good… but he's still here.

He has everything he needs and more, but he no longer seems to enjoy any of it… because others can have it too.

He just knows that we like that Siamese more… but that's not so.

It's a sad thing to see him grow old and bitter, thinking that life has somehow cheated him. He's grasping for things that don't really matter at the end…while rejecting all the things that do.

I'm not finishing so well myself…

Make your own application… you've still got time.

Truthful Love

If the true measure of our faith is how much we love God and neighbor, then the cause for most of our problems in church and society begins with a lack of love for both.

* * *

The reason the Bible says we are to speak the truth in love is because, in doing so, we reflect the image of God who is all truth and perfect love. It also greatly increases our chances of being heard...

Old Wounds

Day 15

Sam is the most beautiful cat I've ever seen. He is a chocolate Siamese and, next to red headed women, I love Siamese cats the most.

Sam doesn't love me back however… he can't.

He showed up on our doorstep with a large, open wound on his underside that looked life-threatening. After he healed, we learned that the breeder had kept him locked in a closet for the first six months of his life… how he was wounded we do not know.

It took many months to convince him to eat inside, even in inclement weather.

It took years to convince him that being petted would not end up in pain for him.

Now, he allows my mom to pet him… but I remind him of

someone who hurt him and he won't let me near him. It's not that he isn't intelligent... he knows English because when I curse him for spurning my affection he hisses and turns his regal back to me in royal dismissal.

Sometimes... he forgets the wounds and acts like a cat... he revels in the petting and loudly purrs and prances, lost in feline bliss.

Then, suddenly, he remembers... and claws and yowls cease his reverie and he wounds before he can be wounded and runs.

An old wound defines Sam and, because that wound defines him, he cannot enjoy the love and affection that would be showered upon him if he would only allow it.

He always hurts those who care for him the most.

I remind him of someone who hurt him... badly... but I'm not that person.

I wish he could tell the difference.

I'm not giving up on Sam.

Make your own application.

Love Hurts

Day 16

The terrible shrieking startled and confused me. I was at the computer, deep in thought over the day's events, anesthetized by the purring of the heater fan and the kind of tiredness that makes you numb and deaf.

I bolted for the door to see the big tom stray absolutely thrashing Miss Kitty... fur was literally flying along with other substances I shudder to identify.

I pushed the big tom off with my foot and it attacked me with same vigor it was ripping Miss Kitty with... and went through me to thrash her some more.

It received a more vigorous kick and I sent it flying into the yard, while I instinctively picked up Miss Kitty to protect her from more harm.

She attacked me.

In my eagerness to defend her from further harm, I had touched her where she was wounded... and it felt like yet another attack. She scratched and bit, then using her back paws pushed off hard and propelled herself into the night.

I went back in the house, cleaned up, and pondered the wisdom of intercession.

* * *

Later, as I lay sleeping, a cat crying from the foot of the bed awakened me. Miss Kitty had awoken me to apologize... or so it seemed.

I turned on the light and she slinked up the covers to touch our heads together even though hers had a big clump of ripped out fur sticking to it.

I fed her and gently brushed her out with the hands she had bitten earlier.

We're both torn up, but we're both still here.

Make your own application…

The Most Important Thing

Day 17

Squeak is a very odd cat... but she has taught me some very valuable lessons. None more valuable than the following...

When she fell ill, she refused to eat. The only thing that I could do was hold her and pet her and offer her little bits of food from my hand to try to persuade her to take in nourishment.

Now that's she's feeling better she will eat... but not before I spend time petting and loving her. She will walk up to the bowl full of food and wait... and wait... and wait. She will not eat what is in front of her and ready for consumption.

It is only when I come and sit with her and pet her that she will then have her meal.

Before she wants what is in my hand, she wants me.

She must be loved before she can eat.

She's dependent on me for everything… her food, water, shelter, and medicine but she knows I will provide them. She would suffer the loss of them all to be with me and to know that I love her… and to be able to love me back.

Squeak seems to enjoy her meals, her health, and her warm place to sleep… but I'm what matters to her… more than food, water, medicine or shelter.

She's here for the love and she's willing to wait for it above all other needs and pleasures.

She is an odd cat.

I wish I were that odd.

Make your own application…

Heavenly Company

Day 18

A couple of months ago, my mom's cat, Plato, died after giving twenty years of companionship. The parting was that of a longtime friend and Mom used some of her savings to cremate him and now she keeps his ashes near.

Last night she informed me that Plato had communicated to her recently that he was in a better place, and I allowed that was probably true.

This little vignette will cause no end of consternation for those of you who have written and proclaimed me a heretic for believing that pets go to heaven.

That's pretty much why I wrote it...

I enjoy your consternation and wish you much more consternation, and I hope you consternate yourselves to the point of being too physically impaired to type. That's what I wish for.

I'll repent later.

Much later.

Right at the last second.

While I'm at it...

I wish the same thing for those of you that have recently consigned Steve Jobs, Brennan Manning, Jerry Lee Lewis, (and anyone else who didn't recite the Sinners Prayer and invite Jesus into their hearts in your holy presence according to your holy rules) to the pit of hell, forever and ever may they burn, amen.

According to some of you, most folks are going to hell and you're happy about it.

I don't get to make that call... so I'm going to hope for the best.

When some of you actually get to heaven, the first thing you're going to need is a salve for your chapped butt when you find it's overrun with animals and they play praise music with a heavy left hand on the piano.

That's to say nothing of the surprises you'll have about the people who made it in.

Don't be confused when you see me and my cats sitting close to the speakers... it really is heaven and God does know I'm there.

You're going to have many surprises like that.

The grace of God is broader than you can imagine… or want to. Heaven will be filled with great food, great music, great friends, and the presence of the Lord over it all. Might as well practice for it while you're here.

As always, make your own application…

Hurting Others

The pastor who wounds someone so deeply that they leave the assembly of believers may have committed spiritual murder...

Earning Trust

Day 19

The weather has turned cold here and it's been below freezing at night all week. That means that my felines are coming in from the elements... and staying.

My little princess, Squeak, comes in and delicately eats a small meal, then carefully bathes herself and prepares for bed. She gently slides under the covers and curls up next to me and doesn't twitch a whisker the rest of the night.

Miss Kitty comes in like a storm over the Cascades. She's fat, loud, and brash... lacking in both grace and manners. A more uncouth cat I've never met.

One is almost perfect, one is a really not, but I feed and cherish them both.

Late in the evening, when he thinks I'm asleep, Owl sneaks in the open door to escape from the cold. He comes in just far enough to be able to warm up and escape quickly... about a foot inside, but about four feet from the heater… and the food.

I have freely offered him all that my other furry kids have and he wants it badly… but he is afraid of me.

He knows how to survive in his world, he's not so sure about mine. He's watched me carefully the last few weeks… and watched how I treat his kin. He's seen enough to come this far… what he sees from here on out will determine if he comes all the way in from the cold.

I've already prepared him a blanket and a dish.

Make your own application…

What do you Want?

Day 20

When I figured out what she wanted, I was ashamed.

It's been a brutal couple of weeks for Squeak. It began when the owner she loves and trusts crammed her in into a plastic box, made her ride in that big loud machine, and handed her over to another human.

He poked and jabbed and probed her in what must be unspeakable fashion even for a cat. Stuffed back in the box, another ride, then home.

Twice a day since then I forcefully pry open her little mouth and throw rocks down the back of her throat.

I often miss and have to repeat the process.

She has never bit me, never scratched me, and never protested her treatment through the whole process. She takes her medicine, then crawls even closer.

When she sat staring at me the other day I assumed she wanted some of my dinner. So, I got on the floor and began to pull apart small pieces of chicken to offer her.

That's not what she wanted.

I went and got her fresh water.

That's not what she wanted.

I went and got a saucer of milk, but that was not what she wanted.

I put all my offerings down and contemplated what on earth this cat wanted. She climbed into my lap, curled into a ball and fell asleep purring.

All she wanted… was me.

Despite all the painful things that had befallen her that she cannot possibly understand, she still trusts and loves me. Despite it all, she just wants to be in my presence and is content there and nowhere else.

I was ashamed.

Make your own application…

The Cost of Love

Day 21

I feared that that Squeak was sick because she was acting just like my last cat acted before he died. She wanted to be as near as she could to me at all times, forsaking feline dignity because she was afraid herself.

I tried not to think about it… I surely can't afford a vet and surely God would not heap yet another sorrow upon me.

Surely not…

Then, she stopped eating. Then, she stopped drinking. Then, she hid herself away to die in peace.

I went searching for her and the "lady" that lives up the street said that I was describing her cat and her cat was not sick at all and that if I found her to bring her back to her rightful owner.

I found her about an hour later… she had dragged her little body into a sunbeam by the road for warmth and I scooped her up and declared myself the rightful owner… for that right requires love to be valid.

I would sell something if need be... she was going to the doctor.

The doctor examined her and told me he would run some tests, but in his opinion it did not look good... she had obviously had a rough life before she met me... and how would I want to dispose of the carcass?

I loaded her back in the cat carrier to await the results at home. We sat in my chair and I wept until her fur was wet as we groaned together with the rest of the creation.

He called back the next morning. She was very sick, but not necessarily sick unto death. He gave me a plan, he prescribed medications, and he presented his bill.

My conclusions are thus:

Love, at some point, will require payment the lover can't afford.

True love requires sacrifice.

True love pays.

Only the lover willing to pay the price is worthy to be loved.

Make your own application... it's worth the cost.

Room Enough for Two... or More

Day 22

Hot... cat... vomit. That was what I stepped in and what enabled me to slide gracefully head first into the door and grace my forehead with a nice welt.

Once again, one of the cats had made itself sick by repeatedly gorging itself, as if the famine of Revelation was starting tomorrow.

They both do it and they both end up ralphing all over something my bare foot will find. They also fight... mainly over proximity to their Father.

Squeak sleeps on my right side, the immense Miss Kitty on my left... if tails touch, the fur flies... usually about 3:15 AM.

Little Squeak has now taken over my chair during the day... I sit on the edge so as not to crush him, for he will not be moved from this rampart.

Both think they have sole rights to my presence and affections. Both believe that my care and gifts belong to them alone. Both refuse to believe that I'm large hearted enough to care for and feed them both.

As a result, neither enjoys my company, both are miserable, and I'm not having a real good time myself.

They weary me... I will not choose one above the other and I won't stop caring for one because it offends the other one to see another cat blessed. If they understood me, they could relax and enjoy feline bliss at the hands of a benevolent dad.

The problem is that my world has incomplete communication with theirs... if they really could understand me, they would know they are loved and there is more than enough room in my world for both.

Make your own application...

Life in Christ

Which Kingdom?

Christianity isn't about transforming human kingdoms into "godly" ones, it's about ushering in the kingdom of God. We are here to speak truth to power, not acquire it.

Michael Newnham

Fragile Life

Day 23

Just a quick word this morning... a word that I hate.

Fragile

For the second time in as many years, the Lord has showed me that in every way possible, we, I... am fragile. For the second time in as many years I will be having surgery to repair something torn or broken.

Before I submit my body to the surgeon for repair, I need to submit my soul to the Great Physician. Because I have always believed so strongly in the strength of my flesh I ignored the increasing pains and obvious problems in both body and soul.

I could take it... I could handle it.

Maybe not...

Both have now gone under the knife.

I have been assured by both the surgeons, earthly and Great, that I will recover. Both have also assured me that I should have taken care of these problems long ago.

One has told me that this will be an ongoing process... and

surgery is less painful when you stay still.

    Just a word to the wise and tough… you're fragile too.

Make your own application…

New Holiday Needed

Day 24

We need a new Christian holiday. We need to establish some day in every year that the people of God set aside for repenting of relational offenses and seeking forgiveness. We could make as big a deal out of it as we do Christmas or Easter…plan for it, get our lists ready so to speak, and then enjoy the relief and joy that comes through restored relationships.

We can call it "Restoration Day."

Yes, I know we're supposed to do this every day… but we don't.

Just as Christmas gives folks who aren't bent to expressing love an excuse to do so, "Restoration Day" could provide the prideful with an excuse to get right with God and others. Since we have talked so often on the blog about badly dysfunctional and abusive situations in the church family, we've receive many more stories- almost daily.

How much better for the kingdom and those involved would it be if repentance and forgiveness were the hope instead of having to write a book or a blog post to resolve the situation?

"Restoration Day" will never get on the official calendar… but it really needs to be on mine and yours.

Today?

Make your own application…

Looking Back over Your Life

Day 25

I'm reading John Stott's last book… last as in final, not most recent. The beloved Anglican wrote this from the nursing home he now lives in and its contents include his instructions for the disposition of his library when he dies. These are Stott's last thoughts that he wanted to share with the church he has served so well.

It's called *The Radical Disciple* and that is a perfect description of Stott's pilgrimage. It's a great little book, full of wisdom and love written with the winsomeness that is part of all Stott has done. The book is intended to help us live likewise.

Unfortunately, I'm not John Stott.

I'm not a radical disciple… sometimes it's hard to tell if I'm a disciple at all. I despair of ever being Stott-like, let alone Christ-like.

The downside of reading a lot of books about great men of God is that they are constant reminders that you are not one of them. If I wrote a final book it would be called *The Guy Who*

Michael Newnham

Barely Made It and Got In Smelling Like Smoke.

Not really... even though it would be true from my perspective.

From God's perspective, the same blood covers me and brother John and He has given me the same robes of righteousness that Stott will soon be clothed in.

That, my friends, is stunning truth.

The ground is level at the foot of the cross.

That... is the Gospel.

No one preached it better than Stott; nobody needs to hear it more than me.

It's truth... it's true for you as well... even if your walk looks more like mine than John's.

Make your own application...

Moving Forward

Day 26

I would never, have never, will never, arbitrarily tell someone suffering that it's time to "move on" from what they are grieving. Moving on implies that one is expected to go on from a given point forgetting the wounds and damage done to them.

That's like telling someone with a broken leg that they need to get up and dance.

Moving forward is not the same as **moving on.**

People moving forward recognize the damage, acknowledge the pain, suffer the loss… but refuse to be defined or enslaved by the acts perpetrated against them. Part of my "pastoral" responsibility is to help people bind their wounds, get the swelling down, get crutches that fit and move forward in their faith and in their lives.

When we're able to do so, we move from being victims to being overcomers… and overcomers inherit the kingdom.

You don't "overcome" good stuff.

We move forward in faith, never forgetting the sin, never forgetting the victims… but moving forward, believing as we go, that God has not forgotten either.

We move forward, believing that God uses all things for our good and His glory, even the sins of wicked men and the pains of living in a fallen creation.

We move forward, believing that our good Father never wastes our tears and that there is always a holy purpose in our pain.

We move forward, knowing that He may not reveal that purpose in our lifetimes.

We move forward, with absolute faith in the sovereignty, holiness, righteousness and love of our God.

We are not moving on; we are moving forward, in the power of the Holy Spirit.

That's my mission, that our commission, that's where we will find our purpose and our hope.

Make your own application…

Growing in Knowledge

Day 27

> Therefore, beloved, since you are waiting for these, be diligent to be found by him without spot or blemish, and at peace.
>
> And count the patience of our Lord as salvation, just as our beloved brother Paul also wrote to you according to the wisdom given him, as he does in all his letters when he speaks in them of these matters. There are some things in them that are hard to understand, which the ignorant and unstable twist to their own destruction, as they do the other Scriptures.
>
> You therefore, beloved, knowing this beforehand, take care that you are not carried away with the error of lawless people and lose your own stability.
>
> But grow in the grace and knowledge of our Lord and Savior Jesus Christ. To him be the glory both now and to the day of eternity. Amen.
> (2 Peter 3:14-18 ESV)

I have held to wrong doctrine at times in my Christian journey. Rumor has it that I hold to some now.

Paul can be hard to understand and Jesus doesn't always answer in black and white or yes and no.

I've never held to any damnable error, but error is error.

I'll never have it all down and neither will you or anyone else.

That's because we're not home yet… we're growing. Growing in the grace and knowledge of our Lord. We started with a limited understanding at one point and we move past that point and keep growing in our understanding until we are glorified.

We see in part…

What I would have wrote or preached ten years ago would sound different today… I thought I had it down then.

Now… not so much.

I affirm the creeds and confessions common to the church and understand beyond those that there will be places of disagreement.

We can disagree on these secondary matters with one of two attitudes toward each other… either with an attitude of love and openness to searching the Scriptures together or one of suspicion.

One will be blessed of God to bring light; one will bring division and strife.

One facilitates growth; one damns the same out of fear.

Fear produces anger, anger produces strife and division.

I don't have to fear being wrong… Jesus forgives that and He promises that if I follow Him I'll end up right in the end.

> There is no fear in love, but perfect love casts out fear. For fear has to do with punishment, and whoever fears has not been perfected in love.
> (1 John 4:18 ESV)

We love each other when we allow for growth, when we disagree with grace, and our only objective is truth.

Make your own application…

The Focus for Church

The more you study church history the more you understand that when the church leaves it's place of speaking truth to power and desires instead to share the power, the church ceases to speak anything that power doesn't want to hear.

* * *

Pastoral care is like parenting. You can choose to focus on what's wrong or you can choose to focus on building up what's right. One way will lead to joyful maturity, the other to someone who grows up looking for the faults of others. We need to be as vigilant about commending growth as we are about confronting sin.

You're Not Stupid

Day 28

Dear brethren,

I have one message for you this morning:

You're not stupid.

You're not weak, vulnerable, emotionally and intellectually unstable people who need to be protected from ideas by religious authorities.

You're sheep of the Great Shepherd and He says that you will hear His voice. You are indwelled and sealed by the Holy Spirit and have been entrusted to the care of Jesus Himself.

He says He'll lose none of those the Father gives Him.

That includes you.

There's nothing to fear… even from the bad guys.

> Children, it is the last hour, and as you have heard that antichrist is coming, so now many antichrists have come. Therefore we know that it is the last hour.

Michael Newnham

> They went out from us, but they were not of us; for if they had been of us, they would have continued with us. But they went out, that it might become plain that they all are not of us.
>
> But you have been anointed by the Holy One, and you all have knowledge.
>
> I write to you, not because you do not know the truth, but because you know it, and because no lie is of the truth.
>
> Who is the liar but he who denies that Jesus is the Christ? This is the antichrist, he who denies the Father and the Son.
>
> No one who denies the Son has the Father. Whoever confesses the Son has the Father also.
>
> Let what you heard from the beginning abide in you. If what you heard from the beginning abides in you, then you too will abide in the Son and in the Father.
>
> And this is the promise that he made to us—eternal life.
>
> I write these things to you about those who are trying to deceive you.
>
> But the anointing that you received from him abides in you, and you have no need that anyone should teach you. But as his anointing teaches you about everything, and is true, and is no lie—just as it has taught you, abide in him.
> (1 John 2:18-27 ESV)

There are folks who would deceive you.

They're easy to spot.

They leave the Body ("they went out from us") and they deny that Jesus is the Christ.

It's that simple.

There, the ODMs (online discernment ministries) can retire... we don't need them now.

God promises that the Holy Spirit will guide you, Jesus will protect and keep you, and the Word will inform you of the truth.

Stay in the Body, stay in the Word, and feel free to jump any traditional fence you please.

God will keep you inside the only fence that counts.

Make your own application...

Michael Newnham

Things I Thought

Hearing God

The voice of God speaking through creation is called "natural revelation". It is only when I am able to hear that voice that I can lay aside all the unnatural ways we have to live in these days. In other words, get off the computer and go outside...

* * *

When you pray for guidance assume you're being led even if it appears you're going nowhere.

* * *

Prayer would be a lot easier if you got a delivery notice when you were finished...

Michael Newnham

Be a Hero

Day 29

There is a new biography of the late Chicago Bears running back Walter Payton coming out next week. In it, we will learn how the football hero known as "Sweetness" was a drug addict and adulterer and a bunch of other unsavory things that we really don't need to know.

According to the biography's author, "There's something important about learning that even the greatest among us have their burdens. Whether you're a Hall of Fame running back or a guy moving cement, we all have issues. No one lives up to the pedestal... The goal is to find out who he was and how he lived. I'm very defensive about that. You want to write an honest and accurate biography."

One more hero bites the dust.

I wasn't a Payton fan... I'm a Viking and he killed us. He was tougher than steel with a will to match... indomitable. He was great with the fans, great with charity, great on the field.

Now we know he wasn't a hero in many other ways.

This is what we do now… we celebrate people; we build them up… the higher the better… because it's so satisfying to tear them down when we're done. We remember the dirt and the salacious details of their sins and the rest falls by the way.

Oddly enough… the Bible does this in reverse.

In the Older Testament, we meet the heroes of the faith warts and all.

In the Newer Testament, God applies Compound W wart remover to the same folks.

In Hebrews 11, Noah sobers up and becomes an "heir of righteousness"… Abraham isn't willing to give up his wife to save his backside, Sarah isn't hating on anyone, Jacob isn't a heel snatcher, Samson isn't a whoremonger and, well, you get the point.

The shame-laden sinners become heroes of the faith in the Hebrews Hall of Fame.

> But as it is, they desire a better country, that is, a heavenly one. Therefore God is not ashamed to be called their God, for He has prepared for them a city. (Hebrews 11:16 ESV)

These days we build you up, then tear you down and shame you... God tells the truth about His people, then lets them know He's not ashamed to be their God.

God is not ashamed to be called their God... make your own application...

Changes Around Us

You can go home again... but you will inevitably be reminded that it's no longer your home.

* * *

The most difficult thing that "I think about" is how to hold on to what I believe are biblical truths, while having great empathy with people who believe those truths persecute them.

Symbols

Day 30

Symbols are a very important way that we communicate in society and culture. The best symbols bring out of us not just recognition of what is being signified, but an emotion about it.

> The American flag.
> The twin towers.
> The Nazi insignia.
> The cross.

All of these not only encapsulate some truth or event, they bring forth in us an emotional feeling about that truth or event.

People become symbols as well… and symbols by their nature are not complete biographies or treatises, they simply evoke a truth and an emotion.

> JFK
> MLK
> Elvis
> Disney

All of these names evoke something in us… I reveal my age by my choices.

I was five when JFK was assassinated… and I will always

remember the grief and the silence that enveloped everyone in this country for reasons I didn't understand.

I don't recall long dissertations on his foreign or domestic policy; I remember people laying down their differences to grieve the loss of the American Camelot.

All of the "real" men behind those symbols were lesser beings than their symbols became.

We know the dirt now and there is much of it… yet we keep what they symbolized in our hearts because it was good, and good for us to believe in.

Steve Jobs and Apple were a symbol of something good to millions of us and we grieve at the loss. We know the dirt; we know that the products we love are made under hellish conditions where workers are exploited.

So is almost everything I own and wear.

To be as consistent as my critics want on issues of social justice, I would have to sit in my yard, half-naked except for the woven hemp gunny sack, and send this article out by smoke signal.

We live in a world where the global economy is exploiting the least of these… and Apple is part of that global economy.

There is a time to talk about those things… I've brought it up on my blog more than once. That time is not when people are mourning the loss of a symbol… that spoke of great deeds and great things to aspire to.

> For everything there is a season, and a time for every matter under heaven: a time to be born, and a time to die; a time to plant, and a time to pluck up what is planted; a time to kill, and a time to heal; a time to break down, and a time to build up; a time to weep, and a time to laugh; a time to mourn, and a time to dance; a time to cast away stones, and a time to gather stones together; a time to embrace, and a time to refrain from embracing; a time to seek, and a time to lose; a time to keep, and a time to cast away; a time to tear, and a time to sew; a time to keep silence, and a time to speak; a time to love, and a time to hate; a time for war, and a time for peace.
> (Ecclesiastes 3:1– 8 ESV)

My final thought is about my favorite symbol… the cross.

Because of the cross I don't have to be consistent… He was.

Because of the cross I'm free to love those who are less than they seem… because I am as well and He does too.

Because of the cross, one day no other symbols will be needed.

As always, make your own application…

Grace

You can assess how much you believe in the grace of God by determining how much you want the person you despise the most to receive it.

* * *

Some people in the church ration grace as if they paid for it themselves... and act as if, should they spend what they have, it will result in personal loss.

Priorities

Day 31

When I saw the candy apple red Buick filled with older matrons pull up across the street, I knew that either the Jehovah's Witnesses or Avon were about to descend on the neighborhood. It was the former, and I watched as four of them extricated themselves from the boat-on-wheels and went around to help a fifth Witness out. They lifted her up and handed her first cane, draped a black handbag across her other arm, then gave her a second cane... and dispersed.

Listing badly to starboard from the weight of the bag, moving the canes twice for one step forward, she headed... for my driveway.

It was painful to watch her labor so much to make such little progress so I decided in my chivalry to meet her halfway... to reject her efforts to evangelize me and inform her that she was in a cult.

I have a heart of gold, but I'm a busy man.

I greeted her and she steadied herself enough to reach into

her bag and start to pull out some literature, which I quickly informed her she could keep as it was cultic and I hoped she would hear and receive the Gospel.

I also noted to myself that she would have to hear it somewhere else, because I was already running late and I should have just locked the gate in the first place.

Naturally, she told me I was lost and jammed one cane into the ground in front of her, stabbed the pavement to the side with the other and began the difficult process of turning around... and going on to the next place that would summarily reject her as she worked her way toward hell.

For just a moment, I was possessed by the spirit of Rob Bell and hoped that maybe Jesus would have mercy in the afterlife on someone who worked harder to cross the street for what she believed than I do in a month believing in Him.

We all know that won't happen. I'm lazy and self-obsessed, but my theology is right, thank God.

* * *

After getting cleaned up, I headed to the convenience store to get a bag of ice before we went to the skate park. To my surprise, a clerk who had quit months before had returned, preferring low wages to no wages.

The only thing that had changed was her hair color (again) and she had added some more ink... and I didn't think that was possible. She is covered in all visible areas (and I suspect the not-visible ones as well) with tattoos.

She cannot ink her eyes though, and her eyes have always said that all that ink was an intricately crafted quilt, a layer of extra protection to try to cover a ravaged soul and a tattered heart.

If I were to pick a perfect candidate to hear and receive the Good News, it would be this gal. Maybe I'll try someday, if I have the time and that old JW doesn't get her first.

* * *

We finally got to the skate park and the kids were huddled about at one end and *he* was on the other. They call him "Jesus on crack" and he does bear a resemblance to that portrait of our Lord that my grandma had… the one of the Caucasian Jesus with the long, soft, brown hair and neatly trimmed beard looking placidly out to something because he has clean hair and is always placid.

The difference is in the eyes… this guy looks like he could have had a pig's-eye-view of the world from inside the pig in Gadarene. He rants and rambles and mutters and I quickly decide how I will injure and disable him if he moves toward Trey.

My only concern was what to do with my iPad if I had to engage in such a confrontation.

Do I drop it, do I save it first… how do I save my iPad?

Jesus-on-crack disappears into the brush and skating resumes, and I'm thankfully spared from my dilemma.

That was my day yesterday before noon… three folks headed for hell, but my iPad is secure and my sermon is finished.

Make your own application…

The Red Letters

Day 32

I have a theory...concerning spiritual dryness and times "in the desert". There seems to be a large congregation among the cacti these days, and I will offer up a possible reason as well as a potential cure.

Each of our traditions offers **a certain view of God**, and if you want to continue to gather with that certain group you pretty much embrace their view. That perspective never varies much from week to week and book-to-book, so it will be the perspective that comes to your mind when meditating on spiritual things.

They will tell you who God is and what He's like, what He likes and what He doesn't, and in your mind that will create a personality of God that is the God you relate to.

The problem is... that all of those perspectives fall very short of really engaging with who He truly is and what He desires in His relationship with you.

For example, while I was in Geneva among the TRs (Truly Reformed), I learned that in every service it pleases God if we refer to ourselves as "worms" at least once, and follow that confession by loudly "singing" the Psalms without musical accompaniment or a discernible tune.

I asked God about this the first night and He referred me to Calvin's writing on adoption and said that, as soon as they started howling the Psalms, He turned the sound down and asked Mahalia Jackson to sing over the top of them.

Seriously…

My point is that, if this were the only teaching I had about God, I would dry up and blow away from the lack of joy and constant severity. The pews looked like a gathering of people who suffered from severe hemorrhoids, who had come to salute Calvin for being faithful despite his own affliction.

I kid because I care…

Each of our traditions will skew our vision of God in some way, and then those who claim to represent Him will often skew it yet further. Thus, you end up with a god made in the image of man and those gods are very easy to walk away from and they can never fulfill our need for the real thing. You end up in the desert, wandering about looking for a little shade and enough moisture to keep walking.

Here's the cure: **the red letters.**

Open up a Gospel and deal with Jesus... not doctrine, not theories... just Jesus.

> Long ago, at many times and in many ways, God spoke to our fathers by the prophets, but in these last days he has spoken to us by his Son, whom he appointed the heir of all things, through whom also he created the world.
>
> > He is the radiance of the glory of God and the exact imprint of his nature, and he upholds the universe by the word of his power.
> > (Hebrews 1:1– 3 ESV)
>
> > Jesus said to him, "Have I been with you so long, and you still do not know me, Philip? Whoever has seen me has seen the Father. How can you say, 'Show us the Father'?"
> > (John 14:9 ESV)

Put yourself in the story... wherever it says He spoke to the disciples, put your own name in there because He's speaking to you. Listen to Him... listen to Him rebuke the religious, and let Him confront you all over again with the reality of who your God really is.

Get rattled and afraid and be challenged by His radical ways and His radical demands on you, and then reject all the demands that religious people want to put upon you that He never mentions.

Feel the fire and the pain and the hope of His kingdom exploding into our world and join the revolution.

Spit out the brackish fluid of religion and drink deeply from the well of living water.

He will change you… if you dare.

Sometimes Oswald Chambers just ain't enough…

Make your own application…

Don't Worry

Day 33

Here's a brief story from a few years ago. Our text for church this week is Luke 12... but first a little background. Senate Republicans are using the nation's unemployed as a pawn against the Democrats with mid-term elections coming up. Thus, they have refused to approve unemployment benefit extensions and 1.2 million people have lost this limited income.

In three weeks I will join them and in a month some of my church members will as well.

We're scared... very scared.

(As a side note, the next time I vote Republican will be when hell freezes over and many of the "Christian right" get frostbite.)

It was against this backdrop that we opened the Word.

> "Therefore I tell you, do not be anxious about your life, what you will eat, nor about your body, what you will put on. For life is more than food, and the body more than clothing. Consider the ravens: they neither sow nor reap, they have neither storehouse nor barn,

and yet God feeds them. Of how much more value are you than the birds! And which of you by being anxious can add a single hour to his span of life? If then you are not able to do as small a thing as that, why are you anxious about the rest? Consider the lilies, how they grow: they neither toil nor spin, yet I tell you, even Solomon in all his glory was not arrayed like one of these. But if God so clothes the grass, which is alive in the field today, and tomorrow is thrown into the oven, how much more will he clothe you, O you of little faith! And do not seek what you are to eat and what you are to drink, nor be worried. For all the nations of the world seek after these things, and your Father knows that you need them. Instead, seek his kingdom, and these things will be added to you.

"Fear not, little flock, for it is your Father's good pleasure to give you the kingdom."
(Luke 12:22–32 ESV)

If we take the Word of God literally when the grammar and literary style demand it (and we do), then we have direct commands and promises here that we have to deal with. This passage for us is as much a confrontation as a comfort.

Don't be anxious.

Don't worry.

Don't run hither and thither trying to provide for yourself in the flesh.

Doing these things is disobedience and proof of little faith in residence.

Worry and anxiety shouts to your world that your God could be a deadbeat dad who may or may not meet your needs, depending on His whims and the state of the local economy.

Worry shrinks the soul and closes the heart.

Worry is sin.

Everything I just wrote is true… and I'm still freaking out… with dignity, mind you, but it is what it is.

He knows.

He knows what we need and it's His "good pleasure" to give these things to us.

He also knows that I'm not sure I believe what I just wrote.

I believe, help my unbelief.

It's His "good pleasure" to do that too.

Make your own application…

The Return of the King

If you really believed Jesus could return at any moment, you wouldn't act the way you do. Just sayin'...

* * *

I think eschatology is a much more enjoyable study when you define it as Jesus coming back to bring heaven and earth together, instead of Jesus coming to catch lazy virgins who need an oil change.

Waymaker

Day 34

When Pharaoh drew near, the people of Israel lifted up their eyes, and behold, the Egyptians were marching after them, and they feared greatly. And the people of Israel cried out to the LORD. They said to Moses, "Is it because there are no graves in Egypt that you have taken us away to die in the wilderness? What have you done to us in bringing us out of Egypt? Is not this what we said to you in Egypt: 'Leave us alone that we may serve the Egyptians'? For it would have been better for us to serve the Egyptians than to die in the wilderness." And Moses said to the people, "Fear not, stand firm, and see the salvation of the LORD, which he will work for you today."
(Exodus 14:10– 13 ESV)

It will be two years next month… I was in Geneva. I had not thought about ever going to Geneva… such a thing was so far from my reality, it was incomprehensible. I had certainly not prayed for such a thing… I'm usually consumed with finding enough daily bread for everyone.

I certainly didn't deserve such a gift, nor could I have earned it in this lifetime.

No, my going to Geneva was an act of unthinkable,

incomprehensible, utterly unexpected, completely over the top, grace mediated from the hand of God through the people of God.

Which brings me (circuitously) to our text for the day. The Hebrew children were between a rock and a hard spot…actually between an army coming to slay them and a sea waiting to drown them.

This is a metaphor that "resonates" with a lot of us here.

They were terrified and angry with God.

That resonates too.

God showed up… not early, not late, but right in the nick of time and right before about bunches of them were going to have heart failure anticipating their fate.

He did something they hadn't anticipated, could never have anticipated, would never have anticipated… and they walked across on dry ground.

In front of me is a dark sea that threatens to drown me, and in back is an enemy who would push me into that darkness.

I'm going to keep my peace and wait for the unanticipated

grace of God.

I've seen it before.

Make your own application...

Pastoral Buzz Words

As I study the Scriptures I've yet to find a passage that speaks to the necessity of "growing your church."

* * *

Do not use the term "vision casting" if I'm close enough to spit on you.

What is God Doing in your Life?

Day 35

> The book of Job is not only a witness to the dignity of suffering and God's presence in our suffering but also our primary biblical protest against religion that has been reduced to explanations or "answers". Many of the answers that Job's so called friends give him are technically true. But it is the "technical" part that ruins them. They are answers without personal relationship, intellect without intimacy…On behalf of all of us who have been misled by the platitudes of the nice people who show up to tell us everything is going to be all right if we simply think such and such and do such and such, Job issues an anguished rejoinder. He rejects the kind of advice and teaching that has God all figured out, that provides glib explanations for every circumstance. Job's honest defiance continues to be the best defense against the clichés of positive thinkers and the prattle of religious small talk.
> Eugene Peterson (from the introduction to the Book of Job, in THE MESSAGE)

I have this acquaintance…who I avoid like the plague…who always greets me with "what is God doing in your life?", then waits for an answer. I have no idea what God is doing in my life at the moment, and neither does anyone else.

Nor do I have a clue what He is doing in anyone else's life.

Job had the temerity to ask God what He was doing…and God informed him in no uncertain terms that it was none of his business.

Same answer I've got on more than one occasion.

Sometimes when God is at work it feels good, sometimes it feels like hell. It's God, no matter what it feels like.

Your job, my job, isn't to discern what God is doing or to judge someone's reaction to what God is doing. Our job is to mourn with those who mourn and rejoice with those who rejoice and leave the quality control issues to the One who is at work.

I'm working on losing the arrogance that presumes the ability to discern God's purposes for others, and the hardness of heart that judges how they are doing in those purposes…because I really don't have a clue.

Make your own application…

The Gift of Rebuke

Day 36

With one adroitly turned and timed sentence, I had nailed my adversary and cyber-slapped him silly. I was beside myself with glee. Anticipating further opportunities to whack him, I bundled up my iPad and took Trey to the skate park where he could skate and I could scorn, and a good time would be had by all.

Then the iPhone rang.

It was a very good friend who I assumed was calling to congratulate me on my cyber-slapping and share in the mirth. In reality, he was calling to rebuke me, and to rebuke me before there was more to rebuke me for.

He reminded me of my own stated commitments about how we communicate on the blog and, more importantly, of the Scriptures I claim to be subject to.

I was rebuked and rebuked soundly… and it was a gift from God.

I want to celebrate the gift of rebuke today and talk about the giving and receiving of the same.

The first thing I want to tell you is that, if you are wise, the Bible says you'll hear and understand a rebuke.

I have a small circle of friends…and all of them know that they can, should, and are expected to honestly rebuke me when necessary.

It's an act of love.

God speaks through the people that He places in your life…and a rebuke from your loved ones will spare you from the discipline of God, when you are willing to listen.

> A rebuke goes deeper into a man of understanding
> than a hundred blows into a fool.
> (Proverbs 17:10 ESV)

Rebukes are part of God's sanctification process… as I noted, a good rebuke heard from the heart saves you from God's discipline, which is much less pleasant to bear than the momentary embarrassment of a loving rebuke. The person who won't receive them is indeed a fool… and many blows are forthcoming.

> It is better for a man to hear the rebuke of the wise
> than to hear the song of fools.
> (Ecclesiastes 7:5 ESV)

We all have a choice when rebuked… we can receive it as the voice of God or we can justify ourselves by claiming persecution to our personal rooting section.

It is way too easy to enlist a chorus to sing to us the song of fools, who keep us from correction and guarantee future discipline from the hand of God.

David understood this principle… when Shimei stood by the road hurling rocks and insults, David's team wanted to chop his head off to shut his mouth.

David was wise…

> But the king said, "What have I to do with you, you sons of Zeruiah? If he is cursing because the LORD has said to him, 'Curse David,' who then shall say, 'Why have you done so?'"
> (2 Samuel 16:10–11 ESV)

David's men were singing the song of fools, but David was listening for the voice of God.

> Better is open rebuke than hidden love.
> (Proverbs 27:5 ESV)

Love that is unwilling to correct or be corrected isn't love at all…it is proof of a lack of love.

I thank God for those who care enough to rebuke me… who do you have in your life that loves you enough to do so?

Do you love them enough to hear?

Make your own application…

Hating the Brethren

Day 37

By this it is evident who are the children of God, and who are the children of the devil: whoever does not practice righteousness is not of God, nor is the one who does not love his brother.
(1 John 3:10 ESV)

We know that we have passed out of death into life, because we love the brothers. Whoever does not love abides in death.
(1 John 3:14 ESV)

So we have come to know and to believe the love that God has for us. God is love, and whoever abides in love abides in God, and God abides in him. By this is love perfected with us, so that we may have confidence for the day of judgment, because as he is so also are we in this world. There is no fear in love, but perfect love casts out fear. For fear has to do with punishment, and whoever fears has not been perfected in love. We love because he first loved us. If anyone says, "I love God," and hates his brother, he is a liar; for he who does not love his brother whom he has seen cannot love God whom he has not seen. And this commandment we have from him: whoever loves God must also love his brother.
(1 John 4:16 –21 ESV)

There is this "brother"... who I despise. I mean I really can't stand him and at times have considered driving a very long way just to hit him in the mouth once.

If finances allowed, I'd like traveling to hit him to be a regular part of my schedule.

However, being vaguely familiar with the verses posted above, I've tried to repent and work on this.

I've tried to please God by trying not to hate this brother as much.

I've tried to please God by telling Him that I know that He doesn't like this guy much Himself.

I've tried to please God by informing Him that I really don't hate the brother, I just pity him for being such an ass.

I've tried to please God by assuring Him that, if this brother would just confess to being the ass we both know he is, I would condescend to being civil in my thoughts and words toward him.

As a last resort, I've agreed just to ignore the aforementioned brother as an act of Christian charity whilst savoring my contempt for him.

I have yet to please God in this matter.

God calls us to love and not as a suggestion… He says over and over again that one can base their assurance of salvation (or lack of) on the disposition of their hearts toward the brethren.

He also says that we can measure our love for Him by the same.

I don't like those verses, but every time I send them to Him for editing and clarification He sends them back the same way.

It will take an act of God to get me to love this brother… and I think that's the point.

I keep telling Him I want to see Him move in my life… I just want to pick where… and how.

It's within the realm of possibility that, to see God move where we want, we must first allow Him to move where we really don't want to see Him at all.

Possible…

Make your own application…

Grow in Grace

There can be no "grace" without an "offense". If you want to grow in grace, then you have to be sinned against early and often. Being offended is either an opportunity to grow in the things of the Lord or an opportunity to exercise the flesh.

Waiting

Day 38

> And while staying with them he ordered them not to depart from Jerusalem, but to wait for the promise of the Father, which, he said, "you heard from me; for John baptized with water, but you will be baptized with the Holy Spirit not many days from now."
> (Acts 1:4–5 ESV)

There are times when all we have is a promise… and an order to wait. That's what the disciples had here… if you think they knew what was going to happen, how God would fulfill His promise, and how it would all work out when He answered, you're wrong.

They received the promise, obeyed the command… and waited.

That's what the pattern still is.

We receive a promise and we are to wait expectantly while living obediently.

It's not easy.

We want it now and we want to tell God how to answer our prayers and fulfill His promises.

Good luck with that.

I don't know how or when He's going to answer my prayers or yours… I do know that He's faithful even when we're not… and we're not.

I do know our times and our lives are in His hands and He is working all things together for our good.

Keep waiting.

How to Finish

Day 39

I've spent most the last two days working on a sermon for a memorial service that I will preach tomorrow morning. It was relatively easy to write, as the deceased was an amazing, wonderful, loving, godly woman. I get to talk about a life well-lived and the things that mattered to her…her Lord, her family, and the people that God placed in her life to love.

She served them all well and faithfully.

She leaves a large empty place in many lives… including mine.

I was struck by what didn't matter… I do not know what political party she belonged to, nor does our church belong to a particular denomination. She never owned a computer… never surfed anything but the morning paper. I don't think she ever heard of Rick Warren or Todd Bentley. The only ministerial scandal was when we accidentally put wine in her communion cup instead of grape juice… she hated the taste of wine.

Her ministry extended as far as the places where she had kin.

Her legacy is a long list of people no one ever heard of, who knew they were loved and prayed for every day she was alive.

She ran the race set before her and paid no attention to how strangers were running theirs.

She changed the known world around her by doing so.

She ran the race, she kept the faith, she finished well.

Go and do likewise.

Live

Day 40

I am hurting... physically, emotionally, and spiritually. I want to have strong drink and scream; I want to cry and fight, cry some more and collapse in exhaustion and relief. I will do none of those things... not really.

You see, I'm a Christian and Christians only do things in moderation.

We are trained to be moderate at an early age.

At puberty, we are told to ignore the wild ravings inside our minds and groins, and to facilitate this we have neutering rituals called "youth ministry" every week. We are told of how dangerous and sinful our thoughts and feelings are, and how they will be changed in an instant to something righteous and holy... just as soon as we buy a marriage license and the man of God mumbles the sacred words... but not one damn second before.

We must be moderate... until we hear the words and then our lusts are transformed.

Some do not wait, and they will be stained for life and bear the scorn of the Almighty... they are slaves to their passions and we will not be enslaved by anything but moderation.

Amen.

Though our forefathers, the Jews, and my closer kin, the Puritans, were earthy and vibrant and loved to party, feast, drink, and dance, we know better...we know the devils that lurk beyond unrestrained joy and immoderate expressions of exuberant life.

We will have none of that; we will not even grieve without restraint.

We will not hire mourners to wail for us, because we cannot express our pain loudly enough at the loss of a loved one... no, we will be moderate. We will not have a funeral or a wake, we will have a "celebration of life" and pretend that it doesn't hurt that much and that we won't forget they were here, and that we will join them sooner than we think.

We will be moderate and dignified and our dignity will please God.

Amen.

I... I am not a good Christian. I want us to have a Mardi Gras, instead of Easter services; I want to howl and sing and mock the defeated enemy of my soul. I want to eat chicken with my hands and feel the sting of good whiskey wash it down the back of my throat. I want to dance with my beloved and lose myself in the scent of her neck and rejoice that God knew what He was doing in the Garden.

I want to celebrate my salvation by a God who was acquainted with sorrow and the need to not run out of wine when you're having a party.

I want to be like the God who stood at a grave and made fearsome sounds of deep anger and grief.

I want to live.

No, I want to be alive.

There is a difference... make your own application.

Michael Newnham

About the Author

Michael is a dad, a cat lover, and a small-town pastor from Phoenix, Oregon. He is best known for his blog **Phoenix Preacher**, one of America's top 200 Christian websites.

He writes about the real life struggles and blessings of being a Christ follower. His style of writing is down-to-earth and easy to read, yet will inspire and challenge you.

Make Your Own Application- Book 1

MAKE YOUR OWN APPLICATION
devotional series

Don't miss any of these titles by Michael Newnham:

Book 1- Cats, Kids, and Christ

Book 2- Work, Woes, and Wisdom

Book 3- Love, Life, and Legacy

Sold by major bookstores and online book retailers worldwide.

Michael Newnham

THE PHOENIX PREACHER
AN ONLINE COMMUNITY OF FAITH

Visit the WEBSITE

Read Michael's latest posts about the Christian life, integrity in leadership, and trends in the church.

He regularly encourages the downtrodden, confronts abusive ministries, and challenges the average reader to push on in their faith.

The **Phoenix Preacher blog** is worth visiting every day.

Regular features

Mondays- Things I Think About

Tuesdays- Linkathon

Fridays- TGIF

Saturdays- Open Blogging

Sundays- Prayer and Praise

www.phoenixpreacher.com

Make Your Own Application- Book 1

Fiction from Reader Hill

FALLEN KING
an Epic Fantasy
Book 1 of the Cirian War Saga

Available in E-Book and Print formats

A fantastic tale of heroes, demons, and a desperate heir. In the land of Na Ciria, an ancient enemy has returned and there are only a few standing against the invasion:

A PRINCE ABOUT TO LOSE HIS REALM
The grizzled and weary Prince Wintron Dabe, longtime heir to the throne, inherits a kingdom on the same day that most of it falls under demonic invaders.

A PRAYER WARRIOR STRUGGLING TO FIND HIS POWERS

Young Afral must face his heritage and his uncertain abilities. He flees those who want to capture him, while trying to reach a people who may reject him.

A WATCH RIDER FACING BETRAYAL BY SOMEONE SHE TRUSTS

The determined Mylana Farsight must lead other Watch Riders on a dangerous mission to warn the land's long-hidden defenders. Dreadhounds pursue her, even as a traitor seeks to learn her secret.

FALLEN KING, an epic fantasy by Eric Lorenzen, is available for immediate purchase. Buy it today from your favorite bookstore.

Content Advisory: This novel contains scenes of war violence, demonic possession, and human sacrifice.

* * *

TRUTH MOCKER, Book 2 of the Cirian War Saga, will be available soon.

Make Your Own Application- Book 1

Non-Fiction from Reader Hill

MARTYRS' PRAYERS
By Duane W.H. Arnold

"*The prayers that Duane Arnold has gathered together are a beautiful compilation of the love of Christian martyrs for their God and the Lord Jesus Christ. This is a book to be sipped and turned to again and again.*
"*Forgive. Love. Seek for the Truth that will give us life and life more abundantly. Trust is the message that these prayers leave with us, a message crucial for our time.*"

        Madeleine L'Engle, author of Wrinkle In Time

"What would you die for?" It is one of the ultimate questions, as we all treasure our lives. Yet, here they are, those who sacrificed their lives for something unseen. Christians who through the centuries have died for their faith and have left to us their prayers. From Stephen who died beneath the walls of Jerusalem in the first century to a young Iranian Christian shot in Tehran in 1981, they continue to speak to us even in their death.

We live in an age of uncertainty, spiritual pluralism and, in much of the western world, material excess. The prayers of the martyrs come to down through the centuries to challenge our assumptions and the "comfortable Christianity" so often delivered from pulpits and television screens week by week. These prayers remind us of the worthiness of Christ and the costliness of the Gospel. We are humbled by the commitment shown and the price paid. We are encouraged by their honesty and their grace. We are inspired by their vision.

Martyrs' Prayers comes to remind us and challenge us in our faith.

Duane W.H. Arnold, PhD, is a church historian and author. He has served in academic and parochial posts both in Europe and America. Arnold has authored numerous articles and books including, The Way, The Truth, and The Life (1982), Francis. A Call to Conversion (1988), The Early Episcopal Career of Athanasius (1991) and Beyond Belief (2002).

Fiction from Reader Hill

ROAD OF LEAVES
an Arthurian Fantasy
Book 1 of the Ways of Camelot series

Available in E-Book and Print formats

Beware, for the Road stirs every night. When the leaves begin to blow, death follows.

Thom must travel the Road of Leaves for his master. He takes the enchanted, leaf-covered route to get to the hidden city of Camelot. As a magician's apprentice he knows a little about enchantments, but when the Road's magic goes wild, he has no idea how to stop it.

He and a few other travelers survive windstorms and attacks, reaching the Isle of Sun. But there he learns that a sorceress has captured Queen Guinevere and severed the Road's link to Camelot. Thom must try to rescue the queen, in spite of his limited skills at magic. Not only is the queen in danger but so is Adele, the young woman who has captured his affection.

He goes back out onto the wind-torn Road, helped by a monk, a mercenary, and some pixies. Somehow, he must fight his way through to rescue his queen and his love, and to stop the attack on the Road of Leaves.

the WAYS OF CAMELOT series

Book 1- ROAD OF LEAVES

Book 2- ROAD OF WATERS

Book 3- CAMELOT OF THE ROADS (coming soon)

Book 4- ROAD OF CLOUDS (coming soon)

www.ingramcontent.com/pod-product-compliance
Lightning Source LLC
Chambersburg PA
CBHW060159050426
42446CB00013B/2904